BRAINPOWER

YOUR BRAIN WHEN YOU'RE SCARED

BY ABBY COLICH

T0015097

BLUE OWL
BOOKS

TIPS FOR CAREGIVERS

Social and emotional learning (SEL) helps children manage emotions, learn how to feel empathy, create and achieve goals, and make good decisions. One goal of teaching SEL skills is to help children understand what is going on in their bodies and brains when they experience certain emotions. The more children understand, the more easily they may be able to regulate their emotions and empathize with others.

BEFORE READING

Talk to the readers about what makes them feel scared and any physical changes they notice in their bodies when they are scared.

Discuss: Think about a time when you felt scared.
What made you feel that way? How did your body feel?

AFTER READING

Talk to the readers about changes that take place in their brains when they feel scared.

Discuss: What happens in your brain when you feel scared?
What is one way you can help yourself feel better when you are scared?

SEL GOAL

Children may struggle with processing their emotions, and they may lack accessible tools to help them do so. Explain to children that changes take place in their brains when they feel strong emotions. These changes can affect how their bodies feel. Certain actions can trigger changes in the brain that help them feel better.

TABLE OF CONTENTS

CHAPTER 1

WHAT SCARES YOU?

Think of a time you felt scared. What caused your fear? Maybe loud thunder scared you. Maybe a large dog barked at you.

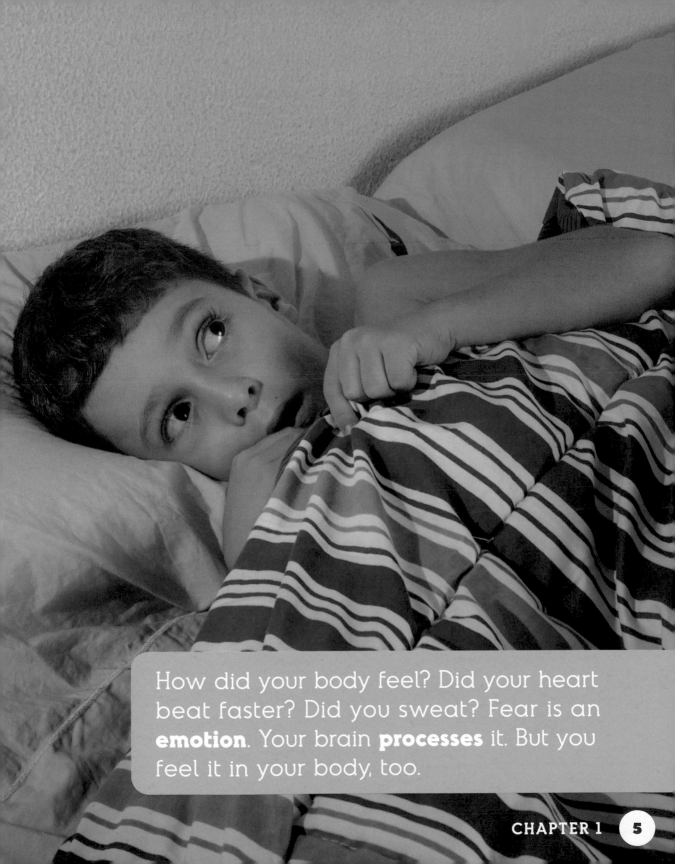

How did your body feel? Did your heart beat faster? Did you sweat? Fear is an **emotion**. Your brain **processes** it. But you feel it in your body, too.

CHAPTER 2

FEAR IN THE BRAIN

When something scares you, your brain works quickly. Your thalamus processes messages from your **senses**.

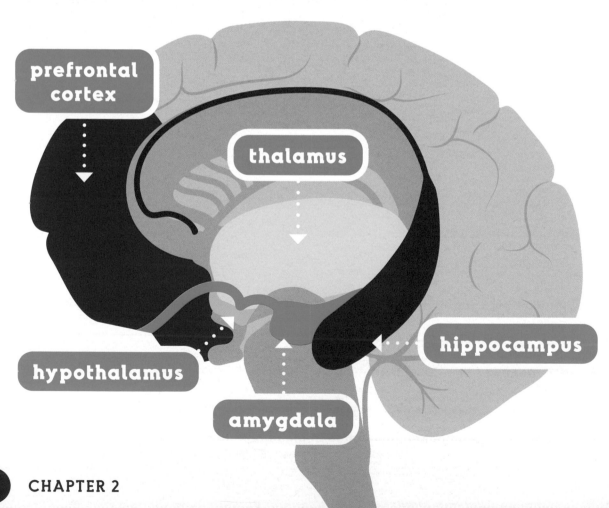

prefrontal cortex

thalamus

hippocampus

hypothalamus

amygdala

If you see or hear something that scares you, the thalamus sees that as a **threat**. It alerts the amygdala.

Imagine you are hiking. You suddenly come to the edge of a cliff. Your amygdala knows you are in danger. You don't have time to think about what to do. Your brain tells you to move back—and quickly.

FEAR OR ANXIETY?

Fear is a **reaction** to what your brain sees as danger. Anxiety is fear of something that could happen. You might be anxious about a math test. If you are worrying a lot about something, ask a trusted adult for help.

In the case of the cliff, the amygdala sees the situation as life-threatening. Then what happens?

1. The amygdala sends a message to the hypothalamus.

2. The hypothalamus sends signals to the adrenal glands.

3. The glands release stress **hormones**. The hormones cause **physical** reactions in your body.

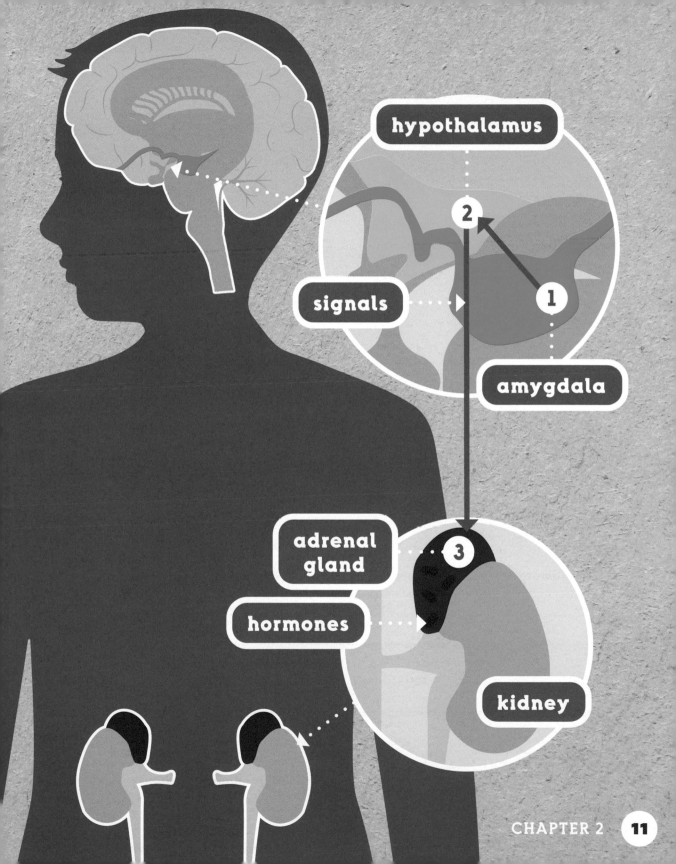

hypothalamus

signals

2

1

amygdala

adrenal gland

3

hormones

kidney

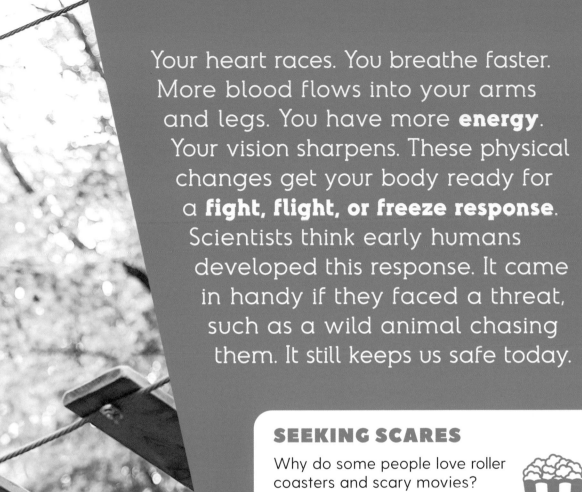

Your heart races. You breathe faster. More blood flows into your arms and legs. You have more **energy**. Your vision sharpens. These physical changes get your body ready for a **fight, flight, or freeze response**. Scientists think early humans developed this response. It came in handy if they faced a threat, such as a wild animal chasing them. It still keeps us safe today.

SEEKING SCARES

Why do some people love roller coasters and scary movies? The boost of energy from stress hormones makes them feel good. They want to do it again!

What happens when something scares you but your brain does not see it as life-threatening? The amygdala alerts the prefrontal cortex. The prefrontal cortex alerts the hippocampus, which is responsible for memory. It compares the current threat to past memories. It sees that this threat is not as dangerous.

For example, imagine you are afraid of spiders. You see a spider, but it is smaller than other spiders you have seen. You are able to quickly calm down.

CHAPTER 3

MANAGING FEAR

It is healthy and normal to feel afraid at times. Fear tells us when we might be in danger. It keeps us safe.

It is possible to **manage** your fears. How? First, figure out what scares you. Then, talk to someone you trust. Studies show that talking about your fears can help you **overcome** them.

Unless it is something that is unsafe, don't **avoid** what scares you. Are you afraid of falling while skateboarding? Learn how you can keep yourself safe. If you are wearing the right gear, you might only get a scrape or a bruise. Skateboard for a few minutes each day until you feel more **confident**.

WHAT IS A PHOBIA?

A phobia is an extreme fear of something. It lasts a long time. You can overcome a phobia. How? Maybe going to the dentist brings on your fight, flight, or freeze response. Watch videos of others at the dentist. This can help you manage your fear.

Make a plan to manage your fears. If you are afraid of insects, think about what you will do the next time you see one. Try taking a deep breath. Then, say to yourself, "It can't hurt me. I will be OK." This will help you take charge of your fears. You will soon feel more confident.

GOALS AND TOOLS

GROW WITH GOALS

Understanding the changes that take place in your brain can help you take charge of your emotions and manage your fear.

Goal: Know what scares you. Make a list of your fears. Think about why these things scare you.

Goal: Research how often the worst possible thing can happen. What usually happens?

Goal: Have a plan. Figure out a method of managing your fears that works best for you.

TRY THIS!

Draw the outline of a tree. On the trunk, write one thing that scares you, like "dogs." Then draw branches. On each branch, list one thing that can happen when you see a dog. For example, your branches might say "attacked," "bitten," "it barked loudly," "it licked me," "nothing." Then think about what happened the last few times you saw a dog. Draw a leaf on the branch for each outcome. Which branches have the most leaves? This helps you see what is most likely to happen when you see a dog. Remember this the next time you see a dog.

GLOSSARY

avoid
To stay away from something or to try to prevent something from happening.

confident
Self-assured and having a strong belief in your own abilities.

emotion
A feeling, such as happiness, sadness, or anger.

energy
The ability or strength to do things without getting tired.

fight, flight, or freeze response
To either prepare to defend oneself, run away, or freeze when faced with something scary.

hormones
Chemical substances made by your body that affect the way your body grows, develops, and functions.

manage
To succeed in something that is difficult.

overcome
To defeat or get control of a problem.

physical
Relating to the body.

process
To gain an understanding or acceptance of something.

reaction
An action in response to something.

senses
The powers a living being uses to learn about its surroundings, including sight, hearing, touch, taste, and smell.

threat
A sign or possibility that something harmful or dangerous may happen.

TO LEARN MORE

FACT SURFER

Finding more information is as easy as 1, 2, 3.

1. Go to www.factsurfer.com
2. Enter "**yourbrainwhenyou'rescared**" into the search box.
3. Choose your book to see a list of websites.

INDEX

Blue Owl Books are published by Jump!, 5357 Penn Avenue South, Minneapolis, MN 55419, www.jumplibrary.com

Copyright © 2023 Jump! International copyright reserved in all countries. No part of this book may be reproduced in any form without written permission from the publisher.

Library of Congress Cataloging-in-Publication Data

Names: Colich, Abby, author.
Title: Your brain when you're scared / by Abby Colich.
Description: Minneapolis, MN: Jump!, Inc., [2023]
Series: Brainpower | Includes index.
Audience: Ages 7–10
Identifiers: LCCN 2022023569 (print)
LCCN 2022023570 (ebook)
ISBN 9798885241496 (hardcover)
ISBN 9798885241502 (paperback)
ISBN 9798885241519 (ebook)
Subjects: LCSH: Fear—Juvenile literature.
Classification: LCC BF575.F2 C65 2023 (print)
LCC BF575.F2 (ebook)
DDC 152.4/6–dc23/eng/20220525
LC record available at https://lccn.loc.gov/2022023569
LC ebook record available at https://lccn.loc.gov/2022023570

Editor: Eliza Leahy
Designer: Emma Bersie

Photo Credits: justoomm/Shutterstock, cover; Anatoliy Karlyuk/Shutterstock, 1; pets in frames/Shutterstock, 3; Krakenimages.com/Shutterstock, 4; Kleber Cordeiro/Shutterstock, 5; Mike Wilhelm/Shutterstock, 7; Aleksey Matrenin/Shutterstock, 8–9; Shutterstock, 10–11; Alla Simacheva/Alamy, 12–13; ER Productions Limited/Getty, 14–15; Anirut Thailand/Shutterstock, 16; wavebreakmedia/Shutterstock, 17; kornnphoto/Shutterstock, 18–19; FG Trade/iStock, 20–21.

Printed in the United States of America at Corporate Graphics in North Mankato, Minnesota.